Protocol
Of
Happiness

Four Lessons On Finding Contentment In Life

Malgorzata Pasko-Szczech

FOR MY SON MAXIMILLIAN
AND
IN LOVING MEMORY
OF MY GRANDMOTHER ZOFIA WANIC

CONTENTS

ACKNOWLEDGMENTS

I would like to thank my friend Marta for giving me permission to use one of her photos of Nature.

All stated opinions represent personal opinions of the Author.

Third party references are provided in the relevant section and the Author would like to express her gratitude to whom the credit is due.

PROTOCOL SYNOPSIS

The essence of Being is hidden in a catalogue of different states of consciousness…

It is the ability to recognise that we are never just one consciousness, and utilise it, that lays the foundation for the often elusive art of Happiness.
In other words, it is the ability to decode and embrace the Art of Being You. You are the key to *your own Happiness*.

And happiness comes from within.

No other person, place or thing can give you happiness. They may give you cause for happiness, but true joy of living (happiness) is a mental ability, which comes from within.
Happiness is a skill, which can be studied, learnt and mastered, but only You can start the journey.
Unhealthy lifestyle and blind conformity are the main saboteurs and Nemesis of Happiness.

America's Founding Fathers came probably as close as possible in defining the relationship between Happiness and each human Being when they declared that all humans are "endowed by their Creator with certain unalienable Rights, that among these are Life, Liberty and pursuit of Happiness". *

Life, Liberty and Pursuit of Happiness…

We can define 'Life' and we can define 'Liberty', but what about *Happiness*?

The clue is in the word 'pursuit' because you cannot define Happiness as it means different things to different people.

It cannot, therefore, be automatically guaranteed.

But we all have the right to our own pursuit of Happiness.

Have you ever wondered if there is a secret formula to Happiness?

There are probably many, and I can certainly share mine in this book.

I believe that Happiness is an Art. A Skill.
So, what does it mean?

Every form of Art is an expression of a particular skill, a very unique expression of each artist.

Therefore, happiness is as unique in its individual meaning as the artist himself or herself.

Five painters will produce five different expressions of the same landscape. Same with sculptors.

Artists study to learn certain skills so they can apply those skills to find their own unique expressions of their talents.

And if happiness is a skill, then like all skills, it can be studied, learnt and improved.

Levels of individual happiness can go up or down, and like any other skill, it needs a bit of polishing and nourishing from time to time.

The main objective of this book is to raise the baseline of your current level of Happiness. Once this is accomplished, you can build on it and nurture it.

Lesson number one is the **'Art of Being You'**, the most important kind of Art as there is no other person like you in the whole world.

You are unquestionably unique, and you need to start to appreciate being you.

But in order to appreciate yourself, you need to first acknowledge who you really are.

Not, who you *sort-of-think* you are, but who you really are.

You probably heard a saying that 'happiness is in your gut' or 'you are what you eat'.

Personally, I could not agree more, so I decided to cover this topic in my lesson number two – **'The Art of Tafelspitz'**.

You will tidy the space around you and discover the **'Art of Enlightened Minimalism'**, so you can focus more on living and being rather than having. This is Art lesson number three for you.

In lesson four, you will stop following crowds and admit that it is perfectly okay to take a break from social influencers (and other pretenders) and discover the **Healing Art of Nature**.

You will come back to the 'Art of Being You' with a clear mind and space around you, with a healthy, nourished body and some free time to finally 'have a go' at being you.

You will no longer behave as the disoriented Alice when she met the mysterious Cheshire Cat:

"Would you tell me, please, which way I ought to go from here?" asked Alice.

"That depends a good deal on where you want to get to" said the Cat.

"I don't much care where…"

"Then it doesn't matter which way you go" …

You will know exactly where you want to go.

LESSON 1:

THE ART OF BEING YOU

The Art of Being You

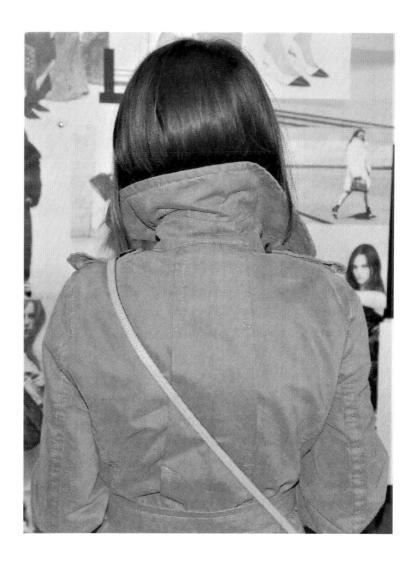

The question came unexpectedly as it had no relevance, not even remote, to the post I applied for:

- *'If you had a chance to be born as someone else, who would you like to be and why? Think of a person you admire and are inspired by.'*

My reply was equally unexpected, I suspect:

'I could think of two women at this moment who have either shaped my life or contributed in some ways to me being the kind of person I am today.

My first choice would always be my grandmother Zofia Wanic, who played a crucial part in my upbringing after my father's tragic death.
To this day, I see and analyse the world largely through her eyes.

I never met my second choice – Simone Veil [1], who was a prominent French politician, French Minister of Healthcare and who became the first female President of the European Parliament.
I read her books twice and I know I am going to read them again.

Their lives were also tragic.

Zofia lost most of her family during WW II, her infant son died shortly after he was born and her whole life was always slightly overshadowed by a deep nostalgia for the era long gone.

As a teenager, Simone survived Nazi concentration camp where her parents and brother were murdered.

Both women prevailed despite having to confront and overcome unimaginable catalogue of life adversities.

Both women could not possibly be more different, and at the same time, both have secured permanent place in my heart and mind.

But would I want to be one of them?'

- *'These are great examples. If you could choose one of them, which one would it be?'* – comes the prompt…

'If I truly have to choose, well, I would like to be born always as **me**.'

They did not even pretend to hide their disappointment; it was all over their faces.

'I am quite happy being me, because…'

I was not given the chance to expand on my answer.

And yes, you guessed it, I did not get the job.

It was however a turning point in my life, because it made me realize that there must be some sort of justification behind this kind of questions.
There must be a general assumption that we are unhappy in our own skin and always either aspire to be someone else (mild case) or fantasize and pretend to be a person of our dreams (severe case).

Well, I am happy and content with who I am.

And I have just shocked the interviewing panel by admitting to such crime.

This book is the fruition of that interview.

'Know Thyself...'

'Know thyself' is one of my favourite aphorisms.

No other two words spell out in such concise way what is the essential element (the keystone if you like) of the foundation of happiness.

To 'know thyself' is to look deep into your soul and be able to display on the outside what is a mirror reflection of your inner self.

To 'know thyself' means having such deep understanding of who you really are that every single decision you make is automatically in harmony with what you truly desire.

To reach this level of self-awareness, you must analyse every aspect of your life and ask yourself; 'is this truly me or am I pretending to be someone else?'

You have to focus more on your internal thoughts, feelings and moods. Only then, you will be able to master the elusive art of happiness.

Remember that it is never too late to change direction and start being yourself.

Artists do it all the time.

Picasso did.

Not many people are aware of the fact, that Picasso, known for his cubism of course, started his artistic

career with a strikingly realistic style.
Just google 'View of the Port of Valencia' from 1895 or 'First Communion' from 1896 and you will understand.

'Know Thyself' vs Be Yourself – what is the difference?

It is not always possible to 'be yourself', you may say.

Yes, and No, I would reply. So, let's explore this further...

The concept of 'knowing thyself' has been studied and referenced extensively by many philosophers.
It is essentially the ability to determine your own behaviour and feelings without being emotionally affected or restricted by outside influences.

Since we are not alone in this world, some level of conformity will always be part of our daily life.
We are, after all, part of a family, community, society...

Good example would be a company dress code or school uniform – you know that this is not truly you, nevertheless you comply with the requirements for a few hours a day.

When you 'know thyself', you will instantly recognise if it is time to conform or not. And you will know right away if it is the right time to 'Be Yourself'.

Remember that you have **the Right** to the pursuit of Happiness and living your life to the fullest.

Here are some of my thoughts to help you start:

1. Don't disregard your past – learn from it! You are not heading in that direction, so consider your past to be like a lesson from which you embrace what serves you and politely disregard what doesn't.

2. Always measure yourself against your own 'normal', not someone else's. What others perceive as 'normal' is merely an opinion.

3. Re-read the lessons as many times as you need and utilize the 'notes' sections – these are all tools to help you develop a stable sense of your true self.

I am from the 'Carl Rogers school of thought'... His "self-actualization" is my pursuit of Happiness, his "self-concept" – my Art of Being Me. Let's conclude this lesson with my favourite quote from the master himself:

"As no one else can know how we perceive, we are the best experts on ourselves"

(Carl Rogers)

LESSON **2**:

THE ART OF TAFELSPITZ

The Art of Tafelspitz

In October 2016, I found myself in Vienna attending a clinical trial symposium. Our host, University of Vienna, have organized a dinner at the renowned Plachutta[2] restaurant and the main dish was Emperor's favourite – The Tafelspitz.

It was my first time at this famous place, but it was not the first time I had Tafelspitz.

My memory went back to my childhood and my grandmother cooking this beef soup dish almost every Sunday.
When I think of family dinners, I fondly recall my childhood and Tafelspitz.

Sitting there and staring at the food in front of me, I was both tearful and excited at the same time.
I took photos of my dinner and I now call it my 'ratatouille[3] moment'.

So, what does the Tafelspitz have to do with happiness?

Nothing and EVERYTHING at the same time.

Tafelspitz represents a traditional dish going back to the Austrian Empire, which is as popular today as it was during Emperor Frantz Joseph's reign.

This simple dish is a testament to the ingenuity of local cuisine, and a lesson in how food can shape our wellbeing.

We are literally, what we eat.

Few months later, I came across a very special book by anthropologist Stephen Le and was taken on a culinary journey to discover what a "100 Million Years of Food"[4] can teach us about happiness.

How different food affects different people and why we should stick to eating traditional cuisine enjoyed by our ancestors.

The following arguments are especially convincing (emphasis added):

"In studies, traditional diets typically do at least as well as nutritionist-approved low-fat, low-salt diets in maintaining health. In part, this is because **the functions of dietary fat, cholesterol, and salt throughout the body are numerous**, while nutritionists have necessarily devoted their limited time and resources to narrow views on the harmful effects of these substances."

Mother Nature always gets it right after all.

Le explains further:

"Traditional eaters didn't bother with scientific studies; they cooked and combined food in ways that maximized their health. The older the cuisine, the better: Five-hundred-year-old-cuisines are a good starting point, because at that point industrially processed foods had not yet made significant inroads into people's diets".

"Traditional cuisines were moderate in fat, cholesterol, and/or salt and therefore tasted good; thus getting ourselves to stick with these diets in not difficult".

And this is why the Tafelspitz that my great-grandparents enjoyed circa 1900, is the same Tafelspitz I enjoy today.

I must confess, I never thought about my dietary habits until I read Le's book.

I now believe that my good health is linked directly to what I eat.

I do not follow a specific diet and quite happily venture outside my 'comfort zone' while on holidays or out with friends and family. But I always come back to my staples, which is superbly simple and traditional food, once popular across the former Austro-Hungarian Empire.

What about you?

Your genes carry everything ever needed to process nutrients required to nourish your body.
You must, however, deliver the right elements, not foreign objects in the form of various junk food.

If you are a vegetarian or a vegan, think what your grandparents would choose; a vegetable stew cooked from fresh produce you just picked up at a local market or a pre-packed gluey something advertised as 'vegan'…

Start eating whole foods and avoid the processed stuff.
It can be your game changer!

LESSON 3:

THE ART OF ENLIGHTENED MINIMALISM

The Art of Enlightened Minimalism

If owning a lot of stuff was any guarantor of happiness, Americans would be the happiest people in the world, and all wealthy people would be happy bunnies 24/7.

Except, that there is no such guarantee.

Sadly, our unhappiness is good for business.

We become prime targets of collective advertising of all sorts. And when we feel under the weather, it is very easy to convince us to spend money on things we don't need, but buy anyway, in a mirage-d hope that we can buy happiness, if only for a day.

We end up with cluttered space and abundance of unwanted objects – what is widely recognized as both the symptoms and results of unhappiness.

It is time to de-clutter your life.

Do not worry, I am not going to propose that you get rid of most of your possessions and adhere to strict minimalism from now on.

I want to introduce you to a form of selective minimalism, with a strong emphasis on having just the right amount of everything.

I call it **Enlightened Minimalism.**

You may ask 'what exactly is the concept of enlightened minimalism'?

Well, it links directly to your inner image and projects this image into physical world in how you live, what you buy and even the way you dress.

It links directly to your inner self, because only you know what the right balance is when it comes to things that you want to surround yourself with.

As you develop an awareness of your true self, you will discover what the right amount of everything means for you.

Your home and your appearance will be a testament of the Art of Being You.

Clothes Speak Volume…

Clothes really do speak volume, therefore do not confuse your professional image with your private one.

Most of us have to get up each morning, get dressed and go to work (or school).

You can take the stress out of getting dressed by creating a capsule wardrobe.

If you work five days a week, create five outfits per season — you will wear each outfit just about four times a month (in case you are worried about being seen wearing the same clothes).

Develop a consistent style of dress and always look professional, this will help you to convey self-confidence and make you feel invulnerable.

Find your signature item and wear it often. It can be something as simple as a souvenir bead bracelet from your favourite holiday.

Exercise **Joy-per-use** attitude.

Most people are familiar with the cost-per-use approach to justify their costlier than usual purchases.

I want to propose a fresher perspective so you can do something for your overall wellbeing — my concept of **JOY**-per-use attitude.

There are the weekends, holidays or just days off work — few more reasons to channel your inner self.

Allow your favourite colour to take care of your wellbeing.

We are constantly surrounded by colour and they play a powerful role in influencing our daily lives.
And most of the time, we are not even aware of this phenomenon.

Wearing your favourite colour will instantly elevate your mood and self-esteem.

…And Your Home is Your Castle

It is time to instill some modern take on this proverbial expression.

We spend about a half of our entire life at home. Our home should be our fortress to which we gladly retrieve, which we enjoy and in which we find contentment.
Therefore, what is just the right amount of stuff at home in the context of our enlightened minimalism?

Which items should you keep?

What new things should you buy?

How much should you really de-clutter?

A study conducted by University College London found that looking at things, which we find beautiful makes us happy. **Start with those.**

When I walk into my living room, my eyes always rest on framed sheet of Beatrix Potter stamps, even if just for a few seconds. These are a very special gift from my son.

When I look up from my laptop screen right now, I see our family photo taken few years back during one of our most memorable holidays.

I have many framed photos, but I do not display them all at the same time. Too many items next to each other create a blurred wall of decorative wrongness.

I like my favourite things to stand out, so they have to take turns being displayed.

Look around your home, room by room, wall by wall, and imagine your **ideal** home. Then act upon the image on the screen of your mind – keep all the things that make you feel happy and get rid of things you do not want anymore.
Make space for things you still plan to buy.

"Other people might want a Ferrari, but I wanted a butterfly house. I built it together with a blacksmith. We designed it together." – *Andre Rieu*

The Beauty – Happiness Connection

"Beauty is the promise of happiness" - *Stendhal*

Can beauty be a function of our Happiness?

Can it truly contribute to our well-being?

I mentioned on the previous page about a study conducted by the University College London and their findings that looking at things, which we find beautiful makes us happy. Numerous other studies reached the very same conclusion: finding beauty in normal activities and surroundings can bring happiness.

But what is beauty?

If I asked ten people to bring to their minds a picture of something they consider beautiful, it is very likely it would be a very different image for each one of them.
That's the voice of perception wanting to be heard.

It also means that beauty is nothing tangible.
It only exists in our heads as a pleasant feeling, but it can, in a subtle way, contribute to our wellbeing.

So, what is beauty to you?

LESSON **4**:

THE HEALING ART OF NATURE

The Healing Art of Nature

We live in a highly paced world, and our need to demonstrate to this world how busy we are is painstakingly clear from numerous social media posts:

'X is attending an event near you...'
'Y is travelling from... to...'
'Z is sleeping' – I have not actually seen this one yet, but it does not mean it is not out there.

We live in an era in which, if you do not have Facebook/twitter/Instagram account, you do not exist.

The fear of missing out is always present, so we keep posting and posting and updating and following.

Occasionally, we are unnerved when we discover that our favourite influencers are being paid handsomely to promote things to us, but we also quickly forgive them and almost by default bounce back into 'following'.
And conforming to whatever is the latest mass obsession.

But how authentic are our responses if this conformity is brought about either by a desire to 'fit in' or a desire to be liked?

Remember that **the Nemesis of Happiness is Blind Conformity...**

Now, imagine that the World Wide Web is about to undergo a global maintenance and there will be no internet connection for a whole week.

Yes, no internet anywhere in the world for a week.

What would you do every day for 7 days?

Do you know yourself well enough to answer this question?

I really hope that your answer to the question posted above **would include spending more time in nature.**

Spending time in nature offers undisputed benefits to both our mental and physical wellbeing.

A simple walk in the forest or park improves mood by reducing feelings of stress, anger or anxiety.

It is a place where we can turn our attention inwards and focus on our thoughts and feelings.

Nature is always there, and always ready to support us.

Spending time in nature is **essential if you are truly committed** to self-discovery and perfecting the art of happiness.

And it doesn't take much to create our private little green oasis...

Photo credit: Marta Cyzio

How Does Your Garden Grow?

"We need to raise awareness of just how much gardens have to offer, how important they are to our quality of life.

They can offer physical health through getting people outdoors and active, spiritual wellbeing through the calm that a connection to nature brings, and cultural richness through their design and 'stories' that they tell.

And the best thing about these amazing assets?

As a resource, they are simply so accessible as they are all around us, from little window boxes, to pockets of greenery on street corners, to public parks to large visitor attraction gardens, we all have the opportunity to see and even make a garden."

Linden Groves[5]

Wild orchid at The RSPB Rainham Marshes Nature Reserve, U.K.

PROTOCOL NOTES

DESIGN YOUR OWN PROTOCOL OF HAPPINESS

PROTOCOL *NOTES*

May you 'find contentment at the level of the heart...in the presence of the Image of your true nature'.

Knowledge is power.
And knowledge of your true self is the most powerful of all.

Learn something new about yourself each day, so you can write **your own** 'Protocol of the Art of Happiness'.

Happiness is an Art. A skill.

Once you learn how to paint or swim – you will never forget it.

Once you learn the foundations of the Art of Happiness, you can only build on it.

Remember:

"As no one else can know how we perceive, we are the best experts on ourselves" – *Carl Rogers*

Start now.

PORTRAIT OF A WOMAN
(My Notes)

She was a very special woman.

She taught me to love butterflies…

She taught me NOT to accept something as my fate just because that's what is expected of me.

She taught me to 'live in my mind' because she lived in hers. And although she lived mostly in her past, and that gave her comfort, she urged me to 'live in my future'.

To dream… To plan…

She taught me the Art of Being Me.

She was my grandmother Zofia Wanic.

Zofia Wanic in 1930s

There are so many realities within us, all complementing each other and congruent to who we are.

Find Yours.

The Timeless Touch of Chives
(My Notes)

A day without fresh, finely chopped chives is a day when I'm on holidays and enjoying local cuisine.

Unless of course chives are part of that cuisine.

For breakfast: I add chives to omelette, scrambled eggs, or Viennese soft-boiled eggs.

For lunch: I sprinkle finely chopped chives on open face sandwiches, add them to tuna with mayo paste or any salad I fancy.

For dinner: Absolute must for any form of potatoes or to add a bit of flavour to soups – I use chives to garnish chicken or Tafelspitz beef soup.

The numerous health benefits of this humble herb are undisputable; chives are extremely rich in antioxidants, which help fight inflammation, colds and even cancer.

I eat them, because thanks to my grandmother, I love them!

The Art of Your Grandparents' Cuisine
BREAKFAST

The Art of Your Grandparents' Cuisine
LUNCH

The Art of Your Grandparents' Cuisine
LUNCH

The Art of Your Grandparents' Cuisine
DINNER

The Art of Your Grandparents' Cuisine
DINNER

The Art of Your Grandparents' Cuisine
SNACK/SUPPER

YOU ARE WHAT YOU EAT NOTES

YOU ARE WHAT YOU EAT NOTES

Fundamentals of My Beige Minimalism
(My Notes)

Beige Has A Voice...

I put a Trench Coat across my arm
As Stendhal talks inside my mind
Nature forgets her basic shade...

But wait
Beauty is not just in my head
It is so tangible
And so in my hand
As I get married in beige ombré...

This classic tread that runs through my veins
To see the colours as Happiness gates
That pleasant feeling
So very different for each of us
That voice of perception
Wanting to be heard...

Colours speak volume – Can you hear?
They speak through ages
In various shades
They scream in khaki
They whisper in oatmeal beige
As I find my beauty in theirs...

Malgorzata Pasko-Szczech

Fundamentals of **Your** Minimalism

Fundamentals of **Your** Minimalism

Special Objects in **Your** Castle

Special Objects in **Your** Castle

How Does Your Garden Grow? *(My Notes)*

Krasiczyn Castle and garden pond, Poland

I love gardens, all of them - from the spectacular Rothschild gardens of the French Riviera, through my childhood memories of my grandmother's humble countryside rose garden, to inspiring English gardens I have the pleasure to visit these days.

I visit gardens and I collect books on gardens.

Linden Groves is the co-author of one of the most beautiful books on gardens: *The Gardens of English Heritage*.

The below transcript is a re-print from my (then) blog, from March 2015. It is as relevant today as it was over 6 years ago when I spoke to Linden about her magnificent book.

MP-S: The first thought that comes to mind while looking at the photos of gardens featured in your book is that... yes, human and nature can actually join forces and create something truly spectacular. The ingredients are always there, nature is abundant, but what can we do in today's computer dominated world to help people re-discover gardens? And I don't mean preserving nostalgia for the times long gone, but a genuine fascination that would produce new gardens for future generations to enjoy?

Linden Groves: *We need to raise awareness of just how much gardens have to offer, how important they are to our quality of life. They can offer physical health through getting* *people outdoors and active, spiritual wellbeing through the calm that a connection to nature brings and cultural richness through their design and the 'stories' that they tell. And the best thing about these amazing assets? As a resource, they are simply so accessible as they are all around us, from little window boxes, to pockets of greenery on street corners, to public parks to large visitor attraction gardens, we all have the opportunity to see and even make a garden. If we can get people to understand all this, then more value will be attached to producing new gardens, and caring for existing ones.*

MP-S: What is a quintessentially English garden? (and park?)

LG: *England has produced so many different types of garden, but the quintessential are probably the early 20th century gardens of Gertrude Jekyll and her admirers, in which colourful blooms spill over onto romantic pathways, framed with clipped evergreen hedges. But amongst those in the know, England also produced the highly-influential and much-loved landscape park of the 18th century, in which Capability Brown and his followers tore away the formal gardens of earlier periods and replaced them with sweeping grass rolling down slopes dotted with tree clumps and elegant garden buildings to serpentine lakes, creating gorgeous wide views. In 2016 we will all be celebrating the Tercentenary of Capability Brown's death and these fabulous landscapes will get the attention they deserve - www.capabilitybrown.org*

MP-S: You have probably heard this question many times before, but I have to ask: which is your favourite garden and why?

LG: *My favourite garden from the book is Wrest Park in Bedfordshire, England as it contains many different layers of landscape history, ranging from a striking 17th century ornamental canal to an 18th century bowling green, to Victorian parterres, to an almost-too-impressive 21st century playground! But the very best thing about Wrest is the survival of its 18th century formal woodland garden, which is very rare in this country, and offers a wonderful opportunity to stroll down long avenues and discover statuary hidden amongst the trees.*

MP-S: Did you always like outdoors as a child? How do you inspire your own children?

LG: *As a child, I always liked being in the freedom of outdoors and was also very romantic with a big imagination, and as historic gardens come with lots of amazing stories, I guess they enable me to indulge those childhood enthusiasms! I inspire my own children by never forcing them to be interested, but by giving them lots of opportunities to be outdoors if they would like. I like to think I tread a fine balance between not dumbing down, whilst always holding on to a love of silliness.*

MP-S: As a landscape/garden historian, would you ever consider writing a book about gardens of Europe? - That's just an example and 'Gardens of France' would be another one.

LG: *Gillian Mawrey, my co-author on the English Heritage book, is a great expert on the gardens of Europe, and in fact especially France. We originally met and became friends when I was her assistant at the Historic Gardens Foundation, an international charity which publishes a unique magazine, Historic Gardens Review, to bring together lovers of historic parks and gardens across the world. I certainly hope she produces a book on gardens of France soon, as it will be top of my Christmas list!* www.historicgardens.org

MP-S: Any projects currently under way?

LG: *I have just begun work on Experiencing Arcadia, which I am thrilled to be undertaking with a garden history partner-in-crime Dr Clare Hickman. This lovely project was inspired by our frustration that garden visitors today can sometimes be less like reliving the past and more like venturing into a museum. We want to know what it was like to walk around a garden in high-heeled 18th century shoes, or to actually have a banquet in a Banqueting House, so are exploring how digital resources can recapture some of this to give today's garden visitors an insight into the 18th century garden visiting experience, and sparking and inform fresh thinking amongst historic garden managers about new ways in which gardens can be made accessible for the public.*
http://www.outdoorchildren.co.uk/experiencing-arcadia/

MP-S: Thank you.

Your Notes on Nature…

Your Notes on Nature...

The Art of You – *Final thoughts as you start writing Your Protocol of Happiness:*

Research the Art of Your Grandparents' Cuisine. What would be your ancestors' typical breakfast, lunch, dinner, or supper?

Define Fundamentals of Your Enlightened Minimalism. Identify Special Objects in Your Castle.

Embrace occasional solitude so you can look into your soul and truly 'Know thyself'.

Make Nature Your Best Friend.

Remind yourself that happiness is an art, and **you are the Artist**.

Create Your Masterpiece!

Notes

Notes

Notes

Notes

Notes

Notes

Notes

Notes

Notes

Notes

Notes

Notes

Notes

Notes

Notes

REFERENCES

Protocol Synopsis
"Life, Liberty and pursuit of Happiness".
*From the Declaration of Independence text, 4 July 1776

The Art of Being You
[1] Simone Veil (1927 – 2017) – French politician and the first female president of the European Parliament from 1979 to 1983.

The Art of Tafelspitz
[2] PLACHUTTA WOLLZEILE
Wollzeile 38, 1010 Vienna, Austria
Phone: +43 1 512 15 77
[3] In Disney's cartoon 'Ratatouille', food critic Anton Ego tastes stewed vegetable dish ratatouille and is taken back in time to his childhood and his mother's delicious cooking. I refer to my Tafelspitz experience in 2016 as my 'ratatouille' moment.
[4] '100 Million Years of Food. What Our Ancestors Ate And Why It Matters Today' by Stephen Le

How Does Your Garden Grow?
[5] Linden Groves is the co-author of 'The Gardens of English Heritage'.

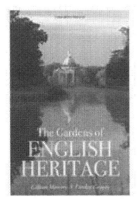

Malgorzata Pasko-Szczech

Expertly
SLOW FASHION

Because Clothes Speak Volume

If time travel was possible, let's say five years into the future, what would you pack to take with you?

Full of beautiful fashion photos, the **Expertly SLOW FASHION** explores the concept of enlightened minimalism and joy-per-use attitude, proving that simplicity is timeless, slow fashion is a mindset and clothes... well, they speak volume!

Dedicated to 'mother Earth', the book points out that so much in our fashion world mimics the unequivocal beauty of Nature. From the iconic colours of a kingfisher copied onto the author's favourite scarf, to the black and white simplicity of an avocet – Nature is rich and so are her colours...

ABOUT THE AUTHOR

Malgorzata Pasko-Szczech is a writer, poet, motivational speaker, healthcare professional working in research, *and an introvert.*
She lives with her family in London, U.K.
Being of Polish and Austrian descent, Malgorzata credits her Polish grandmother for teaching her how to dream and plan, and her Austrian grandfather for showing her how to execute those plans.

Malgorzata is currently working on her *Miscellaneous Art of Being: The World According To Me,* a compilation of thoughts on what is the reality we experience, both the spiritual and material.

Meet the Author: The Introvert Me

Printed in Great Britain
by Amazon